BIBLE VISUALS international

Helping Children See Jesus

978-1-933206-04-2

A Miracle for Samuelito

Based on a true story told by Kathryn Swartz,
the missionary in the story

Author: Rose-Mae Carvin
Review Questions: Doug Stewart
Illustrator: Frances H. Hertzler
Computer Graphic Artists: Ed Olson, Yuko Willoughby
Page Layout: Kelley Moore (pointsandpicas.com)

© 2017 Bible Visuals International
PO Box 153, Akron, PA 17501-0153
Phone: (717) 859-1131
www.biblevisuals.org

A Miracle for Samuelito
Author: Rose Mae Carvin

For a group-setting format of this story and other related items, please visit our web store at shop.biblevisuals.org and search using "5280".

CHAPTER 1

Samuelito (Little Samuel) sat on his heels on the dirt walk in front of a tiny lunchroom waiting for the bus to come. His dark eyes were bright, and his black hair was hidden under the broad brim of his big Mexican sombrero.

As he sat there he watched the blind man at his side. From time to time his eyes shifted to look up the narrow dusty road; yet he knew the blind man would know first when the bus was approaching. *Truly, the blind man sees with his ears,* thought Samuelito.

Soon Samuelito saw the blind man straighten up in his chair, tighten the strings of his guitar and get ready to sing. Narrowing his eyes against the bright sun, Samuelito watched and waited. In a moment the road was one big cloud of dust. In another moment the bus was in sight.

Quickly Samuelito pushed his big hat to the back of his head, tightened his hold on his shoeshine box and walked to the edge of the road where the bus would be stopping.

The bus screeched to a stop and the blind man reached down to make certain his beggar's box was in place. Then he began to sing his sad songs, strumming his guitar as he sang.

Samuelito had a bright smile for each passenger who got off the bus. Of each man passenger he asked, "Shine, Mister?"

But it was one of the women passengers who smiled back at Samuelito and said, "Buenos dias" (Good day).

Something in the woman's smile told Samuelito she was a good woman. He noticed that her teeth were as white and as perfect as his own, and her eyes were as dark as his. Samuelito watched her walk to the side of the bus where the baggage was being unloaded. *Since she is getting her baggage,* he thought, *she is going to stay in our village. I wonder where she will stay?*

Soon all the other passengers came out of the lunchroom and began to board the bus. Samuelito looked with pride as some of them stepped onto the bus with bright and shiny shoes. He had done a good job and he had earned 12 pesos and 65 centavos. *Perhaps I have done better at thees small bus stop than I would have done if I were in a large city,* he reasoned, as the bus pulled away. At least, he did not have to push other boys out of the way and scramble for business. Here, he was the only shoeshine boy.

Happily he counted the money again, then put it carefully in the pocket of his short pants. Pulling his shirt down carefully over his pants, he was getting ready to leave when he noticed the woman standing beside him. "You are not a lazy boy," she said. "Are you saving your money for something special? What is your name?"

"My name is Samuelito, and I hope someday to go to a big city and to school where I shall learn many things."

"That is good," the woman said. "But do you know there is something you can learn right now, if you care to? It is the most important thing in the world for each of us to know. It will cost you no money. May I tell you about it?"

Samuelito was suspicious now. Was this woman after the money he had earned? Did she think she could sell him this little book she held in her hand, or the bigger book under her arm? Well, he would let her talk, *but he would not buy.*

Holding up the bigger book, the woman said, "Do you know about the Bible, Samuelito? It is God's Book and it tells us how to go to Heaven."

"Si! Si!," Samuelito said. "But the Bible, it is not for me to read. I shall learn to read many books, but the Bible, no."

"You can learn to read this little book, right now, because it has no words in it, and no pictures. Yet it tells us the same wonderful story which the Bible tells with words. Would you like to see the inside of this little book?"

"Si," Samuelito said, "but I do not see how it can tell a story if it has no words and no pictures."

"You shall see," the woman answered. "I have told this story to many boys and girls, and many of them have learned how they can go to Heaven when they die."

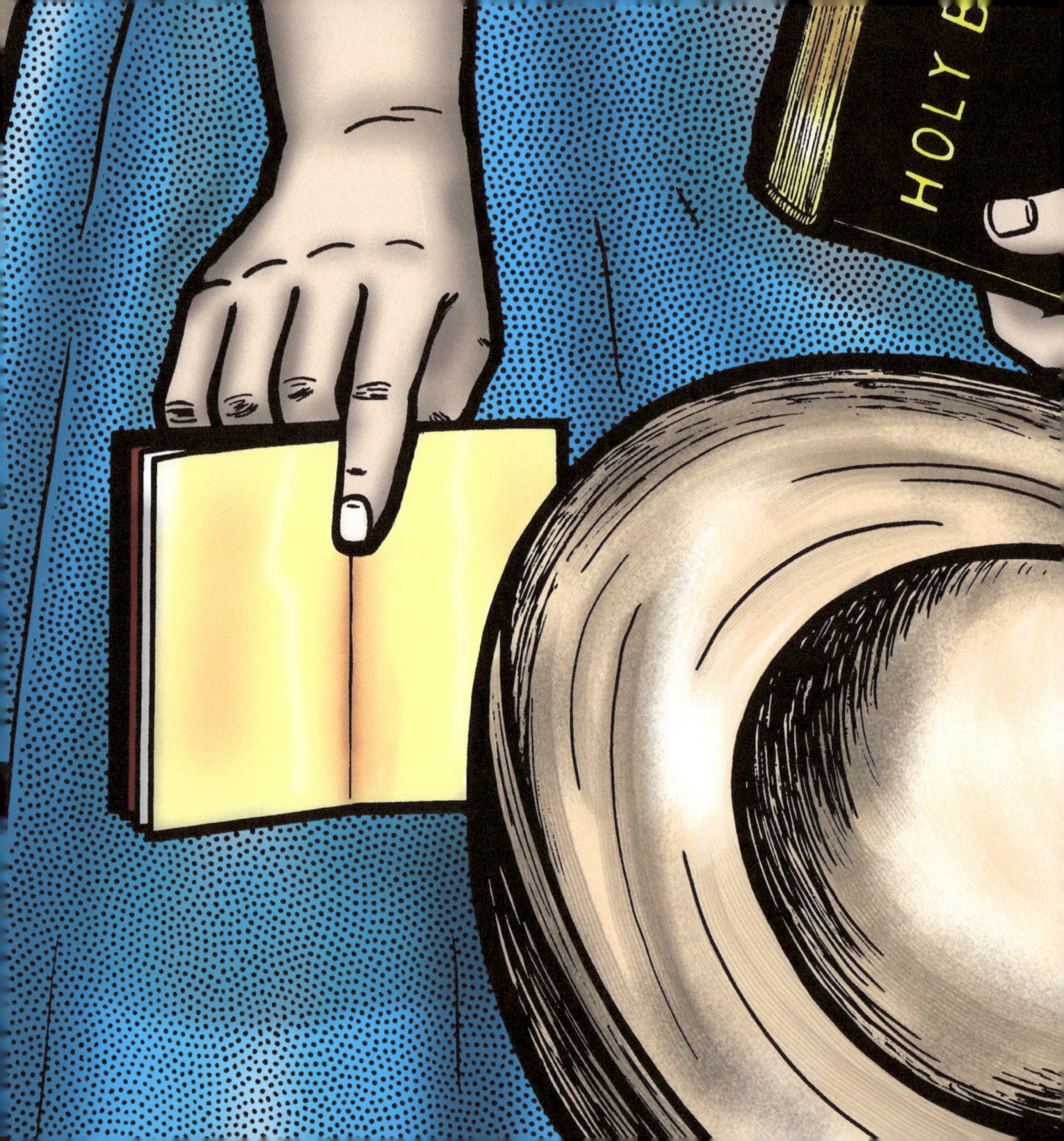

Opening the little book, the woman turned to a page, shiny and gold in color. "This color," she said, "makes us think of Heaven because the Bible tells us the streets of Heaven are made of pure gold." The woman held up the Bible as she spoke.

"We know that Heaven is a wonderful place, where no one is ever sick, and no one ever dies." Lowering her voice, she glanced at the blind man and added, "And no one is blind there, Samuelito." Samuelito felt sorry for the blind man. How wonderful if, when he died, he could go to a place where he could see. The woman continued, "The Bible tells us, Samuelito, that God wants *each* of us to come to Heaven and live with Him someday."

Samuelito lifted eager, dark eyes to the woman's face, as she turned to the dark page of the little book. "This page makes us think of sin," she said. "Sin is wrong things we do, such as lying and stealing."

"But everyone does this," the boy answered with a smile.

"But it is sin, Samuelito. God cannot have sin in Heaven. No one who has sin in his heart can go to Heaven." Samuelito lowered his eyes.

"I said God *wants* all of us in Heaven," the woman went on. "The next page reminds us of the way He has made so we *may* go to live with him when we die, if we will believe and trust Him. All of this the Bible tells us." The woman held up her Bible again.

"This page is red because it speaks of the precious blood of the Lord Jesus Christ, God's Son who died on the cross for our sins. When we trust and believe in Him, He forgives our sins and makes us His children forever. Then, because we belong to *Him*, we shall go to *His* home when we die." Samuelito stared, first at the book, and then at the woman. Could all this be true?

Turning to the white page, the woman said, "This page does not make us think of hearts full of sin, as our second page did. This makes us think of hearts made clean and pure, because Jesus gave His blood for us. Would you like to turn the pages now? See if you can tell *me* what the little book teaches about the Bible."

Samuelito was about to take the book into his hands, when the blind man commanded, "Do not touch the book, Samuelito! It is a trick! What would your papacitos (parents) say to this? I have been listening and I know your papacito will be very angry if he finds out you have been listening to this woman. She is an evangelista (evangelist)!"

Frightened, Samuelito picked up his shoeshine kit and hurried to sit beside the blind man. He loved his father and mother and did not want to bring sorrow to them. Yet this woman could not be bad; of this he was certain.

It was then that Samuelito saw an old automobile stop in front of the lunchroom. "We are sorry to be late," a man said. The man and a woman got out of the car and shook hands with the woman who had been talking to Samuelito. "Let me put your suitcase right in the car and we shall be on our way." Samuelito recognized the couple as a missionary and his wife who sometimes came to the hills of the village where he lived. His father would never allow them to visit in his home.

The woman waved and smiled at Samuelito as the missionary drove off. *She is an evangelista,* Samuelito thought. *She, too, is a missionary. I ought to forget all about the things she said. Yet how can it hurt to think about them for a little? I will never see the woman again.* No automobile could travel the steep, narrow path which led to his home. And this woman would never walk there, of that he was certain. But in his heart Samuelito hoped that she would.

CHAPTER 2

Samuelito quickened his steps toward home. All the while he thought about the dark-eyed woman whom he had met at the bus stop and of the little book with no words or pictures. Something in his heart said that what the colors taught was true. He longed more than ever to be able to read, yes, to read the Bible for himself and to see if these things were really there. How good it would be to know one could go right to Heaven when death came! But perhaps none of this was true. The blind man had said it was not.

Leaving the main road, Samuelito began to climb the steep, narrow path, which led to his home. The little house made of baked mud and a thatched roof came into sight just as the sun began to go down over the mountain. Samuelito hurried. He did not want to be outside when darkness came.

Samuelito's father was already at home. "I have waited to eat with my big muchacho (boy)," he said. "The men of the family must eat together, no?"

"Si," Samuelito kissed his mother lightly, patted the head of his little sister and sat beside his father at a low table.

"And how did our big muchacho do today?" his mother asked as she put red-brown beans on heavy plates.

Samuelito scooped up some of the beans with a tortilla. The thin cornmeal pancake made a very good spoon. Smacking his lips, Samuelito said, "Oh, Mamacita, you will be very pleased. Just you wait and see."

When Samuelito and his father had finished their meal, the mother quickly cleared the table and watched eagerly as Samuelito emptied his pockets. The centavos fell on the wooden table and Samuelito's sister held her hands there so they would not fall off. When the father had finished counting, she and the mother clapped their hands.

"Twelve pesos and 65 centavos," the father said. "You have done well, my muchacho. If you and your sister do as well with the lizards tomorrow as you did with the shoeshine today, it will not be long before you have enough money for this school."

Samuelito's mother took the money then and put it in a big clay crock. She did not try to hide it from the sister. Did they not all try to add to "Samuelito's school"? They would not steal from *him*. From other people? Yes. As Samuelito had told the missionary, this everyone did.

After the house was again made tidy and clean, and the little sister quietly slept in a corner of the room, Samuelito sat for a time in the open doorway with his mother and father. They talked of the happenings of the day. But they talked mostly of the day when Samuelito would be able to go away to school.

"You are nine years old now, Samuelito," his father said. "Soon you should go, or you will be too old to begin. If I sell my pigs tomorrow for good profit, there will be more money for the crock. I work hard. Sister, she helps by selling lizards. Soon there will be enough, no?"

"Si," Samuelito answered, with love in his heart for his father. He wanted to tell his parents about the missionary and what she had said, but he could not. Not yet. For a time it would be his secret to think about, alone. Perhaps later he could tell them.

"Tomorrow we are all up very early," his mother said, as the fire in the little charcoal stove died out. "Now we must sleep." Each went quietly to his own place to curl in a blanket.

Samuelito's father breathed heavily soon after he lay down and Samuelito knew he was asleep. His mother's breathing was less noisy. But because it was regular and deep, Samuelito knew she also was asleep.

Wrapping a sarape (shawl) closely about him, he went again to sit in the open doorway. He sat watching the bright stars in the clear dark sky. Heaven was up there, he thought. Would he and his dear papacitos (parents) ever go there? And the blind man. Could it be that he might also go there and be able to see? If only he could read the Bible for himself, he could find out if these things were true.

Tomorrow he and his sister would go into the mountains for lizards. When they found one they would slip a loop of string around its neck. Perhaps they could catch two each. These they would carry to the main road and hold high for passing motorists to see. Always on Saturdays there were many cars on the road. If he did well they might have 15 pesos for the school crock. And the travelers would have a good lizard dinner!

But Samuelito did not think of lizards for long. His mind went back again to the things he had heard for the first time this day. He had no way of knowing that the Holy Spirit was working in his heart, putting there a longing for the Lord Jesus to be his Saviour.

Back in his place on the floor, Samuelito wrapped himself well in his blanket. He fell asleep, thinking of the woman whom the blind man had said was an "evangelista." Where had she gone with the missionary and his wife? Would he ever see her again? Samuelito fell asleep, dreaming of the little woman whose dark eyes were like his own, and of her friendly smile.

Samuelito was awakened the next morning by the smell of strong coffee and tortillas which were baking in the outdoor kitchen. Rolling out of his blanket, he stretched his arms over his head. "Come and wash before you eat," his mother called from outside. "Your father has already gone to sell his pigs."

Samuelito splashed cold water all over his brown skin, rubbed himself hard with a big towel and combed his hair with the family comb. Then he put on clean shorts and a shirt which his mother had washed in the stream where all the village laundry was done.

As he sat quietly beside his mother noisily drinking sweet coffee and eating the delicious flat tortillas made of cornmeal, Samuelito remembered the time he had been allowed to go with his father to sell pigs. How he had laughed when the ropes, tied one to each pig's hind leg, got all twisted around the pigs and around his father's legs. What a squealing and a grunting there had been when his father untangled them. He had pushed them this way and that with his heavy boot, only to have them tangle the ropes again in a few minutes.

When the buyer had come to look over the pigs, Samuelito's father pushed the squealing animals one by one off the high platform. Samuelito did not think his father was cruel. Pigs did not matter, except for the money they brought.

Samuelito wished he could have gone with his father this day. But he must earn money if that crock was ever to be filled with pesos for his school.

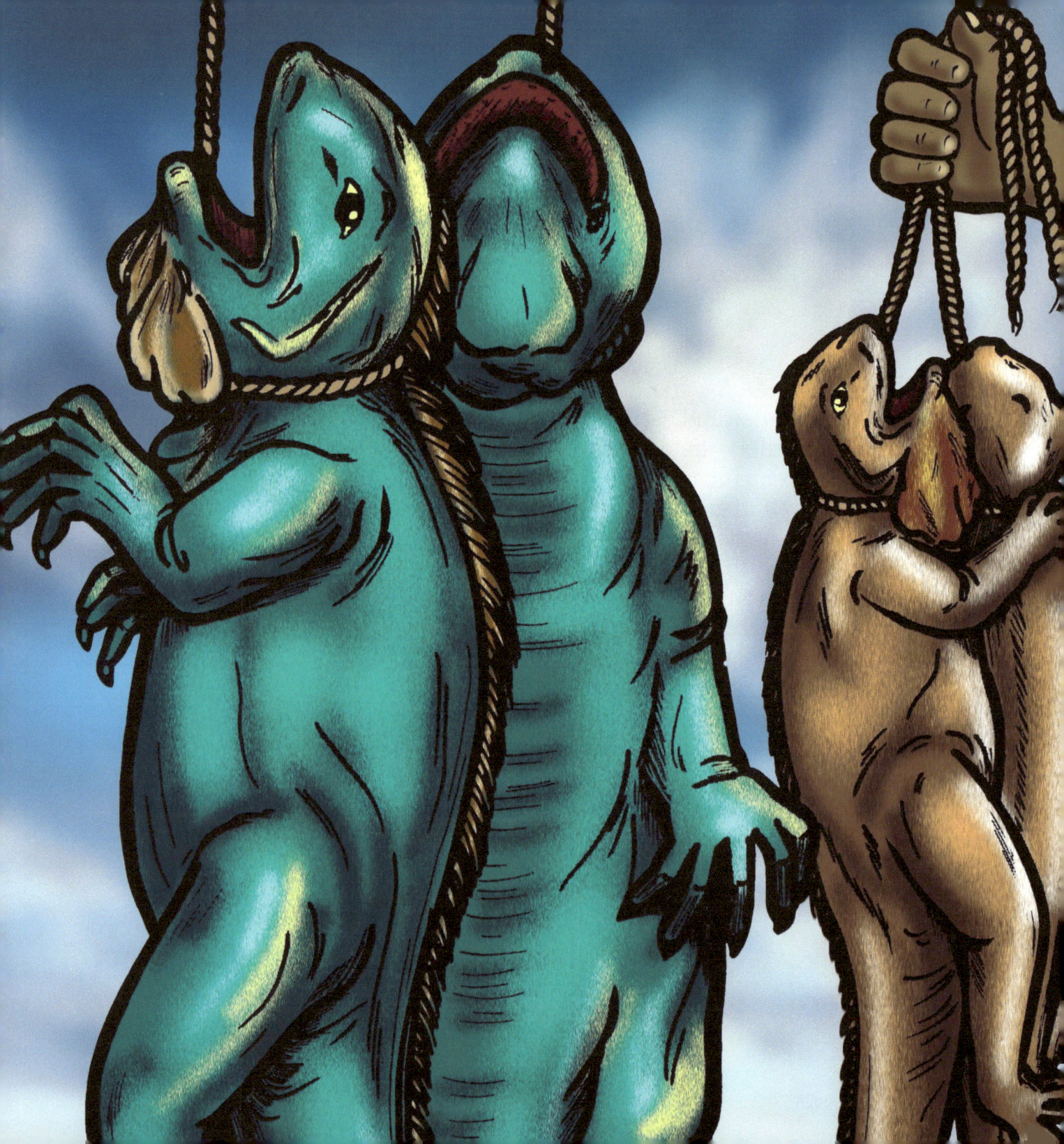

Samuelito and his sister caught two lizards each that morning. They stood on the edge of the highway with the lizards held high on a string for passing motorists to see. Suddenly Samuelito saw the missionary's car coming up the road. As the car came closer Samuelito saw two women inside. One was the woman who had talked to him at the bus stop!

The woman saw Samuelito and waved. Turning, she said something to the driver of the car. The car pulled to the side of the road and she got out. Thinking she had a buyer, Samuelito's sister ran quickly to the woman. Samuelito stood where he was until the woman motioned for him to come closer.

And so it was that, once again, Samuelito heard the Gospel story and saw a Bible and the little book with no words or pictures. He did not know that he and the others made a queer picture standing there in the hot sun. While they listened quietly to the woman, their mouths were opened wide and their dark eyes were opened even wider. They were indeed amazed at the wonderful Gospel message. This time Samuelito told the story back to the missionary for there was no one to stop him.

I shall have to tell my papacitos tonight, Samuelito thought, *for this little nina (girl), she will not be silent.*

CHAPTER 3

Samuelito and his sister sold their lizards for a good price. With the money safely tucked deep in his pocket, the two hurried home. He had little time to think more about what the missionary had said. Samuelito was in a hurry to get to the bus stop before the bus arrived.

Their mother took the money they had earned from the sale of the lizards and placed it in the crock. Having given Samuelito a drink of black, sweetened coffee, she handed him some lunch wrapped in a banana leaf.

With his lunch in one hand and his shoeshine box in the other, Samuelito was off again. He went happily down the road. Each time he earned another peso he felt that the school came a little closer to him.

It was a very weary boy who sat down to eat at the close of that day. But it was not only weariness which made him quiet. He saw that his sister stayed away from him and his mother kept looking at him as though she was displeased.

Finally, when his sister was asleep, Samuelito's mother said, "Now, my niño (child), tell me what has been going on. The little one, she has been talking all the time about a woman who showed you a little book this morning. She said the woman said she had talked to you before at the bus stop. You will tell me now what she said, and who she is."

Samuelito sat down close to his mother. "Mamacita," he said, "I wanted to tell you and Papacito last night. But you hurried us off to bed. Tonight I was going to tell you, Mamacita."

Then, as his mother listened quietly for a while, Samuelito told her the things he had been told. He told her that God's Son, the Lord Jesus, had said that all who believed in Him were born into God's family and belonged to Him. "And that means, Mamacita, that if we trust Him, we shall go to live with Him in Heaven forever when we die. Mamacita, I'd like to . . ."

Samuelito did not finish the sentence. His mother stood to her feet and waved her arms in the air. "Nino," she said angrily, "why did you listen? This evangelista, she is bad. It is not good that you have listened to her. The little one who listened only this morning, she will forget. But you will not forget, my Samuelito, you will not forget."

Samuelito put his arms around his weeping mother. "Oh, Mamacita," he said, "I do not think this is bad. The woman, she is good. I know it is so, Mamacita."

Samuelito's mother was very angry. Because she was, she cried harder and began to shout. "Wait until your papacito comes home tomorrow," she shouted. "He will punish you. Maybe he will say, 'This kind of a son does not go to school!' Maybe he will take the money out of the school crock. You will see, Samuelito, what Papacito will do!"

Samuelito squatted quietly on the floor, his head between his knees, as he waited for his mother to calm down. The little sister woke up and began to cry.

"Be still and sleep!" Then, more gently, "Samuelito, we shall not tell your papa; but you will promise, never you will talk to this evangelista again."

Samuelito did not promise. But his mother did not notice.

"Now we all sleep," she said quietly, as she motioned Samuelito to his blanket in the corner of the room.

Samuelito was up early the next morning. He sat and watched the sun send its rays shooting up over the mountaintop, telling the little village another day was on its way. When a round, red half-circle of sun had appeared, he heard his mother getting breakfast ready. Still he sat quietly and thought—thought of the wonderful things he had heard in the last days. His mother might forbid him to speak to the evangelista, but she could not know his thoughts, so how could she stop them?

His mother came and sat in the doorway with him. "Your papacito should come home soon, Samuelito," she said. "We shall tell him nothing of your wickedness unless you do it again." They sat quietly, waiting until the sun had risen high in the blue sky. When the father did not come, they ate their breakfast.

By noon, the bright sun was high in the sky. Samuelito's mother spoke in a tense voice. "Something has happened to your father. I feel it here," she said, as she placed her hand over her heart. Samuelito and his sister sat close to their mother in the doorway and waited. From time to time the mother stood and, shading her eyes with her hand, looked far down the path.

It was Samuelito who saw the neighbor riding a burro up the path. Never before had Samuelito noticed how slowly the little donkey walked. Breaking away from his mother, Samuelito ran to meet the man.

His mother stood in the doorway too frightened to move. "Something, it has happened to Papacito," she said.

As Samuelito came alongside of the burro, the neighbor said, "My news, it is for your mamacita first, Samuelito." All that Samuelito could do was to run back up the path and stand beside his frightened mother.

The neighbor took his time lowering his feet to the ground. He smoothed his shirt which hung loosely over his trousers and pushed his sombrero to the back of his head. "The news, it is not good, Señora," he said.

"It is my husband?" Samuelito heard his mother ask. "He is sick, my husband? He is—he is—dead?"

"No! No! He is not dead, Señora. He is hurt when he pushes the pigs off the platform. He is tangled in the ropes and the pigs—they pull him off the platform. He is in the hospital, Señora."

It was then that Samuelito's mother began to cry. She wailed louder and louder, wringing her hands. The little sister clung close and wailed as she heard her mother do. Before long, friends from the village arrived to weep with the sorrowing woman and to try to comfort her.

Samuelito did not wail loudly as the others did. No one noticed when he slipped away and hid himself behind the little house. There he sat, weeping quietly.

If my papacito dies, will he go to Heaven to be with God and Jesus? I do not think so because my papacito, he has never trusted Jesus to forgive his sins. My papacito he does not know Jesus died for him. Why did I not tell him when I first heard the story? Why? Because I was afraid! Because I am a coward!

But my papacito will not believe me. He would only beat me.

How do I know this? Perhaps my papacito, he wants to trust Jesus, just like I want to trust Him.

But I have not trusted yet. I have not asked the Lord Jesus to be my Saviour, to forgive my sins, and to live in my heart like the evangelista said I must do.

The Holy Spirit who had been at work in the heart of the young Mexican boy, whispered in Samuelito's heart, "Do it now, Samuelito, do it now."

"Si! Si! Dear God, I do believe that Your Son, the dear Lord Jesus, died for my sins. I want to trust Him now. I want to ask Him to forgive my sins. Please, dear Jesus Lord, come into my heart to live. I want to belong to Your family and go to live with You when I die."

Samuelito sat for a long time thinking of what he had just done. Soon a great happiness came into his heart to keep company with the sadness there because of his father.

Bowing his head way down between his knees, Samuelito prayed again. "Dear God, please make my papacito to live. Help me to tell him about the Jesus Lord. Help me to tell Mamacita and the little sister."

CHAPTER 4

Samuelito's father was in the hospital for many weeks. His back was badly hurt. Neighbors from the village helped the family with food and with charcoal for the fire.

Still, it was necessary for the mother to use more and more of the money from the school crock. Many things were needed for the sick man. Although Samuelito worked hard and earned as much as he could, he knew now that his chances of going away to school were poor.

Samuelito thought often about the mis- sionary and the day when, behind his tiny home, he had been born into God's family. But he became discouraged. Poor Samuelito had no one to teach him more of God's Word. Often he wondered if he had indeed been wicked in believing the evangelista. His mother said he was. She refused to listen when he tried to talk to her about becoming a Christian. The blind man had even said that this trouble had come because of Samuelito's wickedness.

Yet the Holy Spirit had come to live in Samuelito's heart and the boy found comfort in praying. Many times the Holy Spirit led him to hide behind the little house where he had come to know the Lord Jesus, and there to tell his heartache to God.

Whenever Samuelito went to the bus stop to shine shoes, he kept watch for the missionary. As he stood by the highway and held his lizards high, he was looking, not so much for buyers, as for the missionary who could teach him more about God.

One hot, sunny day when Samuelito was very discouraged because the money in the crock was nearly gone, *he saw her*! It was not at the bus stop, nor on the mountain road. Instead, it was as she walked up the narrow path which led to his home.

When Samuelito saw that it was truly the missionary who walked slowly up the path, he ran to his hiding place. He was afraid his mother would be very angry if she found out that this was the evangelista to whom he had listened.

From his hiding place Samuelito watched. His mother and little sister had seen the woman coming. They stood together in the low doorway. Samuelito was close enough to see the bright smile he had come to love and to hear the woman say, "Buenos dias, Señora." His mother scarcely answered, for this was a stranger and certainly not a Mexican. His mother did not trust foreigners.

Samuelito heard the missionary tell his mother that she had learned in the village about the father's accident. She had come to say she was sorry and to see if she could help. She offered his mother a box filled with cookies and candies. Samuelito's mother invited her inside.

It was as his mother and the missionary sat drinking black, sweet coffee and eating some of the cookies, that Samuelito, trembling, finally came inside. He bowed before the visitor and offered his hand as he had seen the foreigners do.

"Señora," the missionary said, "I have met your son before—once in the village at the bus stop and once on the highway when he was selling lizards."

Samuelito saw his mother flash a look of surprise then one of anger. She looked first at the missionary and then at her son.

"Please, Mamacita," he said, "she is good and kind."

The missionary was quick to take advantage. "If you think I told your son wickedness," she said, "why don't you allow me to tell you exactly what I told him? Then, if you still think it is wicked, I'll go back to the village and never talk to him again."

Samuelito's eyes pleaded. His mother didn't like to be rude to this woman who had been kind. "You may tell," she said.

Once more Samuelito sat on his heels and listened to the most wonderful story in the world. This time he understood better. He wanted very much to help tell the story but he was a polite Mexican boy who had been taught to respect those who were older. All he said was a soft, "Si! Si!" as the story was being told. But his eyes were filled with brightness and light. The little sister sat close to the mother and listened. His mother watched from under nearly closed eyelids as the missionary turned the pages of the little book of colors and explained that the colors spoke of truths from the Bible.

The room was quiet when the missionary finished speaking. As she stood to her feet she said, "I must go now before the darkness catches me in the path. Before I go, may I pray for your husband?"

A soft "Si" was his mother's answer as she and Samuelito stood.

Kneeling on the hard dirt floor, the missionary prayed. She prayed that God would make the father well enough to come home soon, and that God would make it possible for Samuelito to go to school. Then she said, "But most of all, dear God, make this dear family come to know Thee as their Saviour and Friend."

Tears were in the mother's eyes when the missionary got to her feet. She did not seem to be angry when Samuelito said, shyly, "I *did* believe and trust the Jesus Lord. I prayed outside, in back of the house. He is in my heart, Señorita! He *did* forgive me."

"Oh, Samuelito, I am glad," the missionary said. Tears were in her eyes now.

If she is glad, then why does she cry? Samuelito thought.

Samuelito," the missionary was saying, "you know the story this little book tells. Here, it is yours to keep. Perhaps your mamacita will want to hear it again. Perhaps you can tell it to your papacito when he gets home. And, Samuelito, I am sure God will answer our prayers and that you will go to school, even though your money is not enough. God can do a miracle, Samuelito. And when you learn to read, you shall have a Bible of your own."

With another smile and a handshake, the missionary was off, calling "Adios" as she went down the path. Samuelito did not know she was going back to Mexico City the next day. He did not know she had been sent by the Holy Spirit that day to his home. But Samuelito *did* know that his heart was again completely filled with happiness. Had not God already done a miracle by keeping his mother from being angry and by allowing her to hear the wonderful story?

Samuelito and his mother and sister stood in the low doorway and watched the missionary as long as they could see her. When she was out of sight Samuelito's mother said, "Si, my son, you are right. The woman, she is good." With her hand over her heart she said, "I feel it in here. She speaks only true words. Will you tell me again the story from the little book, Samuelito, my nino?"

With joy in his heart, and guided by the Holy Spirit, Samuelito went over the story again and again. His mother seemed not to tire of the repetition. "Remember, Mamacita," Samuelito said, "this, it is in the Bible. The little book of colors tells only what is in the Bible. Si, Mamacita, I am sure. My heart, it tells me that this is right."

Before they lay down on their blankets that night, Samuelito and his mother knelt on the floor, just as they had seen the missionary do. The mother asked for forgiveness of her sins, as her son said she was to do. Then she added, "Please, I do not know how to say it, but I know Jesus died for me too. I love Him very much."

Neither Samuelito nor his mother noticed the little sister who knelt behind her mother and repeated the words she heard her mother say. But when the mother got to her feet, tears running down her cheeks, and her arms about her son, the sister drew close. "I did it, too," she said.

The three sat late that night in the doorway, watching the stars and thinking of their new home in Heaven to which they would go someday.

CHAPTER 5

The ambulance, bringing Samuelito's father home from the hospital, stopped on the road where the path to the little home began. It could travel no farther for the path was too narrow. The friends from the village were waiting with a homemade stretcher. Gently they carried the father up the path.

Samuelito's mother had been working all morning getting ready for her husband's return. She swept and re-swept the dirt floor. She cleaned everything she could find to clean even if it was already clean. She gave sweet coffee to the men who had carried her husband up the path.

When they had gone she squatted beside the soft bed she had prepared for her husband. "Does your back hurt very much?" she asked. They hugged each other, both crying and talking at the same time, while Samuelito and his sister watched from a distance.

"It is good to be home," the father said, "so good to be home."

The father motioned for Samuelito and his sister to come close to him. After giving each of them a hug he turned sad eyes to the school crock and then to Samuelito's face.

"Papacito, it is nothing—it is nothing," Samuelito said softly. "It is better that you are going to be well again."

The father turned his head away and closed his eyes. Because he was very weak, he began to sob. "Is it all gone, my son?" he asked.

"No! No! Papacito, it is not *all* gone. And I think I can go to school after all. Maybe there is a way. If you will please sleep, I will tell you about it when it is time. Sleep, Papacito."

Seeing his mother's look of surprise, Samuelito laid his finger across his lips, as a sign for silence.

Turning to her husband, the mother said, "Si, Papacito. You sleep. Your siesta (nap) must be long today, for you have had a hard journey and you must now get well and strong again." Soon the sick man was breathing heavily and they knew that he was asleep.

Samuelito's mother sent the little sister out to play. Then, turning to Samuelito she whispered, "Why did you promise your papacito something when there is nothing to tell?"

Putting his arm around his mother, Samuelito said, "Ah, Mamacita, there *is* something to tell. The evangelista, she prayed that I go to school someday. You have not forgotten? We must tell Papacito. Then when the prayer is answered he, too, will know the woman is good and speaks truth."

"Ah, my nino, my nino." Throwing her arms about Samuelito, his mother held him close. "How can God put money in the crock, eh?"

"I do not know how, Mamacita, but I know He will answer the prayer. Is not our papacito home again? This prayer God answered. I, too, have prayed about the school. He will hear, Mamacita; He will hear."

Samuelito's mother turned away sadly. *My poor boy, he will be disappointed again,* she thought.

Each day Samuelito's father grew stronger. Soon he would be able to work a little. Samuelito went each day to the bus stop to shine shoes. Each Saturday and Sunday he and his sister tried to sell lizards. When they couldn't sell them, they brought them home for Mamacita to roast on the little charcoal stove and they had a fine meal. Always he watched for the missionary—and always he was disappointed.

Each day Samuelito prayed for the schooling for which he yearned. He prayed also that his father might be willing to listen to the story Samuelito longed to tell. As yet his father would not listen to the story the evangelista had told to Samuelito and his wife.

"The trouble we have had," he said, "is it not enough? It is because you have both been wicked to listen to this woman that we have had more trouble. No, I will not listen. More trouble, I do not want."

Samuelito and his mother knelt often to pray when the father was at work. They were coming to understand better that God was their Friend. Little sister always knelt with them.

Often his mother would say, "Oh, Samuelito, we shall not have enough money for school until you are too old."

To this Samuelito always answered, "But God can do a miracle, Mamacita. We shall keep praying. The kind señorita, she will not forget to pray. You will see. When God does the miracle and I go to school, perhaps Papacito, he will listen to the story then. Perhaps he will believe, no?" Samuelito's mother only shook her head. If only her boy could be right about this.

There was another to whom Samuelito tried to tell the story. It was the blind man at the bus stop.

At first the blind man would not listen. Then, because Samuelito was kind to him and often tossed a few centavos in his beggar's box, he allowed the boy to tell him the story.

"You cannot *see* the colors in the little book," Samuelito said. "You must believe me when I tell you about them. If you can believe me, then cannot you believe and trust God, too, Señor? If you will ask Him to forgive your sins and to live in your heart, He will do it, Señor; He *will* do it. And you will belong to God's family, too. And you shall see someday, when you go to Heaven. These things I know, Señor, because the little book tells only what is in the Bible."

Often when the blind man seemed to be sleeping under his big sombrero, he was, instead, thinking of the things Samuelito had said. He would ask the boy to tell the story again. It would be good to go to Heaven and see all the beautiful things Samuelito said were there. Samuelito said the Bible told this. Yes, he would ask the boy to tell it to him again.

But God would never have a man who had been wicked. Was he not blind because he had been so wicked? No, it could not be true that God would forgive him and take him to Heaven when he died. It could not be true.

Gradually, as Samuelito told the story over and over again to the blind man, the truth of God's Word found another home—within the blind man's heart. He also was born again—a member of God's family. Now Samuelito prayed harder than ever for his dear father.

Then one day a group of strange men got off the bus and made it clear that they intended to stay for a while. They waved Samuelito away when he said, "Shine, Mister?" and began talking to some of the men who always hung around the lunchroom.

The blind man stopped singing. Everyone stopped talking and listened with wonder to the things the men were saying. "We will need quite a few," one of the men said. "Do you think we shall be able to find enough men who will be willing to help *our* men?"

"Si! Si! This we will all do, Señor," one of the men answered.

When the men had asked where they could stay overnight and Samuelito saw them go inside the lunchroom, he jumped up and down on his bare feet and slapped the blind man on the back. "Did you hear this, my friend?" he asked.

And in a flash he was off for the path which led to his home, his shoeshine box swinging in one hand as he ran. The dust of the road became a yellow cloud about his black head, and soon he was out of sight.

CHAPTER 6

When Samuelito's mother saw her son racing up the path, she was afraid something terrible had happened—but not to Samuelito, surely. Did ever a boy run so fast?

Dashing into the little house past his mother, Samuelito panted, "Papacito! Papacito! It is happening! The miracle! It is happening!"

Samuelito's father and mother listened as he told them about the strange men who had come on the bus. They were asking, he said, for volunteers to help build a school. "Did you hear, Papacito? A school! A school *here*, Papacito; right up here, higher yet in the mountains. God has answered our prayers! I shall go to school! Papacito, you will trust Him *now*?"

"No, no, my son. It is not possible that a school should come here. The stones and the wood, how are they to get up this narrow path? The ambulance, it could not come up here. A truck, it cannot either."

But Samuelito was not to be discouraged. "I do not know *how,* Papacito, but I know God has answered our prayer. I know He has, Papacito. And He can get the stones and wood up the path."

Samuelito's father smiled at his eager and excited son. "Please, my nino, do not be disappointed. See, the money in the crock, it is getting more and more all the time, no?"

Samuelito shook his head. "There will not be enough until I am too old, Papacito," he said. "But God will do a miracle. Can we help, please, to build this school?"

"Si, si," his father answered, patting Samuelito's head. He would promise. But there would be no school in the hills, of this he was certain.

How surprised the father was when, a week later, he saw oxen and burros pulling loads of steel for a framework and wood for walls and roof up the narrow road. On past the little home they trudged, higher into the hills.

"Samuelito was right! Samuelito was right!" Father said it over and over again. "Samuelito and I, we must go and help. Our boy can go to school, Mamacita! Our boy can go to school."

"Si," his wife spoke softly to her excited husband. "And God, He has made a miracle for our boy, Papacito." The woman spoke truth. "Samuelito will learn to read and to write. Samuelito will learn to read the Bible. Samuelito will be a good man."

Looking down at the happy face of his wife, Samuelito's father said simply, "Si."

Samuelito's father learned that the government in Mexico City had determined that boys and girls who lived in the backlands as well as the city children, should be able to go to school.

Twenty-five big diesel trucks had pulled away from a Ministry of Education warehouse building outside Mexico City. These trucks had carried schools which were all measured and cut, ready to be put up quickly. Where the roads ended, oxen, mules, and burros were to carry the cargo to the villages where no schools had ever been.

The school was built quickly near Samuelito's home and a schoolteacher came to live in their village. Sooner than it seemed possible, Samuelito was going to school each day. It was a long time before his father and mother realized it was true.

Each morning, soon after the sun peeked over the mountaintop, Samuelito, all scrubbed and brushed until he shone almost as brightly as the sun, started up the path. He carried a wonderful school book which he was learning to read, and some tortillas carefully wrapped in a banana leaf for his lunch. Always his mother, father, and sister stood and watched him go. They waved to him as long as they could see his brown hand waving back. Next year little sister would go to school, too. This made their mother and father happy.

Samuelito was fascinated with the sliding plastic windows of the school. He looked in wonder at the water pump, the plastic water tank, toilets, a shower, and many things which he had never seen.

Samuelito's father was willing now to listen to the story his son told him from the little book of colors. But when Samuelito said, "Please, Papacito, will you not also come into God's family as Mamacito and I have done?" his father always said, "Not now, my son."

Late one night, Samuelito woke to hear his father and mother talking. "Si, si," the father was saying, "I would like to kneel and ask God to forgive my sins and to tell him I believe Jesus died for me. But this, it is more for women and children, no? My friends, they will think I am a baby, no?"

"Si, they will think you are a baby. And you *are* a baby if you are afraid of what they think." Samuelito was surprised to hear his mother speak this way to his father. But she was saying more.

"Is it not more important to know you belong to God's family and will go to Heaven when you die? Please, Papacito, Samuelito and I, we want you to be in Heaven with us—the little sister, too. Do not be afraid of what your friends say and do."

When Samuelito saw his father and mother kneel on the dirt floor, he sprang out of bed and knelt beside them. They might need some help with talking to God. They might not know just how and Samuelito wanted no mistakes made. Kneeling there in the darkness of night, another soul was born into God's family—another soul was turned from darkness to light.

Life was not easy for Samuelito, nor for his parents when they let it be known they believed what the Bible taught. Many of the boys refused to play with Samuelito and friends turned angrily away from the parents when they met in the village. Many times Samuelito and his mother cried. Often the father was tempted to fight.

But the schoolteacher was a friend to Samuelito. She read the letters to him which he began to get from the missionary. And the things which she read often made her think long into the nights. Samuelito knew now that the missionary had returned to Mexico City and he might not see her again. "But we shall meet in Heaven, Samuelito," she wrote. Her letters helped the family through discouraging times.

Shyly, one day, Samuelito asked the teacher to write a letter to the missionary for him. He wanted her to know that his mother, father, and little sister were all born into God's family now. He wanted her to know he was going to school.

Samuelito had been going to school for a year. He had worked hard and was able to read a little. Then came the day he would never forget. His father came up the path carrying a parcel for Samuelito. Great was the excitement in the little home as Samuelito tore off the string with trembling fingers.

He unwrapped a book—a book from the missionary. Samuelito's voice, as well as his hands, shook as he saw that the book was a Bible. Quickly he turned the pages, picking out words here and there which he could read. Then he hugged the Book close to his heart.

Although he was afraid that, even though she had been a friend, the teacher might take the Bible away from him, Samuelito showed it to her. "Please Señorita," he said, "you will read, please, some of it to me?"

The teacher had never held a Bible in her hands. She was eager to read it. "Si, Samuelito," she said, "but we must keep the Book hidden. Do not let the other boys and girls see it. I shall come at night and read beside your charcoal fire."

More and more often the teacher came to read. She seemed eager to learn what the Bible taught. Samuelito prayed that she, too, would be born into God's family.

Before long, Samuelito's playmates were kinder to him. Whatever Samuelito had become, they reasoned, it could not be bad. Had it not made Samuelito a good and happy boy?

Surely it had. God had worked a miracle for Samuelito.

Delight thyself also in the LORD: and He shall give thee the desires of thine heart.

Psalm 37:4

United States

Mexico

Gulf of Mexico

North Pacific Ocean

Mexico City ●

Guatemala

Belize

Review Questions

Chapter 1

1. Where was Samuelito working and what was he doing? *(He was shining shoes at a bus stop.)*

2. Why was Samuelito happy to be at a small bus stop and not a large city bus stop? *(At a larger bus stop, there would be many more boys there wanting to shine shoes.)*

3. Why is Samuelito saving his money? *(So that he can go to a big city and attend school)*

4. The lady shared a book with no words and no pictures in it. What was the color of the first page she showed him? What does it make us think of? *(Gold. It reminds us of Heaven, where the Bible tells us the streets are made of gold.)*

5. What about the woman caused Samuelito to believe she was good? *(Her smile)*

6. What one thing did the lady tell Samuelito could not be in Heaven? What color in the little book makes us think of this? *(Sin. The dark page)*

7. Why was the color of the third page red? *(Red reminds us of the blood of Jesus, which was shed for us on the cross.)*

8. What is important about the white page? *(It shows us that we can be made pure through Jesus' blood if we believe in Him.)*

9. What did the blind man say to Samuelito that made him hesitate to listen to the missionary lady? *(The blind man told him that his parents would be angry at him for listening to her.)*

10. How do you think Samuelito felt after the missionary left with her friends? *(He was probably confused because he was told she was bad, but in his heart he knew what she was saying was good.)*

Chapter 2

1. Why was Samuelito's family proud of him when he returned that night? *(He had brought home a good amount of money to save for him to go to school.)*

2. What did Samuelito and his parents talk about? *(About Samuelito one day going to school in a big city)*

3. How old was Samuelito? *(Nine years old)*

4. When his parents went to bed, what did Samuelito think about as he looked up at the sky? *(He thought about the Heaven that the missionary spoke about. He wondered if his parents and the blind man would ever go there. He also wanted to read the Bible for himself so he could find out if these things were true.)*

5. What did Samuelito and his sister go out to catch that morning? How many did they catch? *(They went out to catch lizards. They caught two each.)*

6. Why did Samuelito and his sister catch lizards? *(To sell them to travelers along the highway)*

7. Who showed up as Samuelito and his sister were selling lizards by the highway? *(The missionary and some of her friends)*

8. What did the missionary share with both Samuelito and his sister? *(The Gospel story she shared with Samuelito the day before)*

9. Why did Samuelito know he would have to tell his parents what happened that night? *(He knew that his sister would tell his parents exactly what she had heard.)*

10. How do you think Samuelito felt about telling his parents? *(He probably felt nervous, but also knew it was good news to share, so he may have felt excited to share with them.)*

Chapter 3

1. Why do you think Samuelito's mother was displeased with him? *(His mother was probably upset that he had talked to the missionary.)*

2. Why do you think Samuelito shared why he did not tell his parents about the missionary the night before? *(He wanted them to know that he wasn't being deceptive, but there wasn't much time to talk about it before bedtime. His intention was to tell them the next night.)*

3. Why do you think Samuelito's mother reacted the way she did? *(She was upset because their family believed that missionaries were bad people.)*

4. Why do you think Samuelito's mother threatened him with not going to school? *(They threatened to take away the one thing he treasured most: going to school.)*

5. Why did Samuelito's mother begin to worry? *(Samuelito's father hadn't come home when expected, and she feared that something bad may have happened.)*

6. What happened to Samuelito's father? *(He was hurt by getting tangled in the ropes while pushing pigs.)*

7. What did Samuelito think about when he was weeping over his father? Why do you think he thought of these things? *(He thought of his father not going to Heaven, and how he should have shared these things with him before the accident. He probably thought of these things because he loved his father very much and wanted him to know the story of the Gospel.)*

8. Why did Samuelito feel afraid to share with his father? *(He knew he would not believe him, and would probably be punished with a beating.)*

9. What caused Samuelito to want to pray to receive Jesus then and there? *(The Holy Spirit was working in his heart, and Samuelito wanted to respond.)*

10. What else did Samuelito pray for? *(He prayed that his father would live, because he also wanted to tell him about Jesus. He also asked that God would help him tell his sister and his mother also.)*

Chapter 4

1. Why did money have to be taken from Samuelito's school crock? *(To pay for his father's medical care)*

2. Why do you think Samuelito became discouraged, even after entering God's family the day before? *(He was discouraged that the school money was used for something else; he did not have anyone to teach him more of the Bible.)*

3. Why do you think Samuelito went and hid when he saw the missionary coming? *(He was afraid his mother would know that she was the lady he had been talking to and would become angry.)*

4. Why did the missionary come to visit Samuelito's home? *(To offer help, to bring a box of cookies and candies)*

5. Even though she was a missionary, why do you think Samuelito's mother invited her inside? *(Because she was friendly and had brought them a box of goodies; she had offered to help Samuelito's father.*

6. Why did the missionary offer to tell the story to Samuelito's mother? *(She wanted his mother to decide for herself if the story was wicked.)*

7. What did the missionary pray for before she left? *(That God would make Samuelito's father well enough to come home soon; that Samuelito could attend school; that the family would come to know Jesus as Saviour)*

8. Why do you think the mother was crying after the prayer? *(She was probably very glad to have another person praying for her husband and her family. She probably was sad that she had thought this woman was wicked and now knew that she was not.)*

9. Do you think the missionary showing up that day helped Samuelito's mother believe she was good? Why or why not? *(Yes. She realized that the missionary had a good heart and wanted the best for her family.)*

10. How did Samuelito's mother and sister respond to the story the missionary lady had told them? *(They received Jesus as their Saviour.)*

Chapter 5

1. Why was Samuelito's father concerned about the money in the crock being gone? *(He loved his son very much and wanted him to go to school; he felt badly that the money had to pay for his medical care.)*

2. Why did Samuelito believe that God would somehow help him go to school? *(Samuelito had faith that God could answer prayer because his father came home well—an answer to the missionary's prayer.)*

3. What would Samuelito's family do when he and his sister could not sell the lizards on the highway? *(They would have a nice dinner together.)*

4. What did Samuelito pray for every day? Why? *(For money to attend school. He prayed every day because he believed God would answer his prayers.)*

5. Why did the father still not want to listen to the story Samuelito wanted to share? *(He believed that it had only brought their family trouble.)*

6. Who else did Samuelito tell the story? Why was it important that he share the story with him? *(He shared the story with the blind man. He liked the blind man and wanted him to see, and knew that he would see if he would believe in Jesus and go to Heaven someday.)*

7. Like Samuelito, who should we be sharing the Gospel story with? *(We should be sharing it with everybody we like or love, especially our family, but also our friends.)*

8. What happened because Samuelito told the story to the blind man? Did it happen right away? *(He became part of God's family, but not right away.)*

9. What can we learn from Samuelito's telling his friend the story of Jesus? *(We can learn that others whom we know will also receive Jesus if they believe.)*

10. Do you think Samuelito's faith grew when the blind man received Jesus? How do you know? *(Yes. He began to pray harder for his father to also believe in Jesus.)*

Chapter 6

1. Why was Samuelito so excited? How did his father respond? *(He'd heard that a school would be built near his home. His father doubted that it would really happen.)*

2. Why was Samuelito fascinated with some of the plastic things at the school? *(Because they were things he had never seen before)*

3. What change happened in the heart of Samuelito's father because of all this? *(He was willing to listen to the story of Jesus that Samuelito had been wanting to tell him.)*

4. How did Samuelito's father respond to this story? *(He put off getting into God's family.)*

5. Who played a big part in Samuelito's father believing in Jesus? How did it come about? *(Samuelito's mother helped his father think about things. She told him that believing in Jesus did not make him a baby, and that he shouldn't fear what his friends think.)*

6. Was life better for their family? Why or why not? *(Life was not better. In fact, it became a bit worse because Samuelito's friends would not play with him, and people would angrily turn away from them in the village.)*

7. What did Samuelito and the missionary write to each other about? *(She wrote to him things to think about, and he wrote to her and shared that his whole family had come to know Jesus as their Saviour and Friend.)*

8. Why was Samuelito so excited to receive a Bible? *(He wanted to have one so that when he learned to read, he could read it for himself.)*

9. What can we learn about Samuelito's excitement about receiving a Bible? *(We should also be excited to get to read the Bible.)*

10. Why did Samuelito's friends become nicer to him after time had passed? *(They saw that, whatever had happened to Samuelito, it was a good change.)*

www.ingramcontent.com/pod-product-compliance
Lightning Source LLC
Chambersburg PA
CBHW040748100426
42735CB00034B/53